TRAVELLERS OF THE NORTH

TRAVELLERS
OF THE
NORTH

Fiona Smith

PUBLICATIONS

2022

Published by Arc Publications,
Nanholme Mill, Shaw Wood Road
Todmorden OL14 6DA, UK
www.arcpublications.co.uk

978 1911469 18 6

Design by Tony Ward
Printed in the UK by TJ books,
Padstow, Cornwall

The cover photograph is of
'Voyage from Ireland to Norway'
by Maciej Kauczynski (2008),
a stained glass painting in
St. Sunniva's Church, Harstad, Norway

Arc Chapbook Series
Series Editor: Tony Ward

CONTENTS

I first encountered Sunniva in the Museum of Bergen in Western Norway. Beneath the Gothic sculpture of the tenth-century Irish saint, a plaque informed me that the martyred Sunniva's remains had been "translated" to Bergen Cathedral in 1170. Having been "translated" from Ireland to Norway myself, the phrase had resonance for me. I began to wonder how I could best translate the story of Sunniva, who had voyaged miraculously from Ireland to Norway to escape a forced marriage.

I started to research the story of this Irish noblewoman, a tangible link between my country of origin and my adopted home of Norway. There was little to go on. The Latin *Acta sanctorum in Selio*, a twelfth-century hagiography of Saint Sunniva and her companions, was formulaic and lacking in colour. I wanted to avoid the pieties of the lives of saints and tell the story of a navigator, a sailor and a farmer.

The story of another saintly sailor, Saint Brendan the Navigator, who some believe to have been the first European to reach the Americas, is a firmly established part of Irish cultural heritage. His legendary sixth-century voyage has been celebrated in film, music and literature while Sunniva's sea journey rarely gets a mention. Sunniva, who became the patron saint of Bergen, has been largely forgotten in Ireland outside of the academy. Academic research indicates that her story is part legend, part conflation of the stories of other travelling ascetics – *perigrini* – whose fate was to be martyred, then sanctified. I wanted my poetic reimagining of Sunniva's life to reach beyond this. What if she too had been an early navigator? What did she encounter on the way to Norway? These questions would form the basis for my poems and were the aspects of her story that interested me.

There are many versions of the story. In some accounts, Sunniva is "set adrift" as a punishment for her defiance in the face of her father's demands that she marry a Viking. In others, Sunniva and her followers decide to set sail from Ireland without oars or sails in two boats. Miraculously, the Irish drift northwards to the Western coast of Norway. It has even been suggested that they bobbed along, cork-like. After storms at sea tear the parties asunder, one boat ends up on the deserted island of Selja and the other on the neighbouring island of Kinn. On Selja, the Irish sailors seek refuge in caves and live on a subsistence diet of fish. They are left to themselves, as the mainland Norsemen use the island only for grazing sheep.

However, Sunniva's community attracts attention when scurrilous rumours spread back to the mainland that the Irish settlers are slaughtering and eating sheep. The Vikings come to attack, and Sunniva and her followers hide in a cave. They pray for death rather than confront the barbarians. Their prayers are answered in the form of a rockfall, and they die as martyrs in the cave. Not long afterwards, a beautiful, eerie light is observed on Selja. The recent Christian convert, King Olaf, and Bishop Sigurd travel to Selja to investigate the strange events and they find the body of Sunniva intact. The sanctification process had begun.

Sunniva, the saint, has over the centuries served as a symbol of feminine spiritual purity in Norway's religious and cultural history, much in the way the Virgin Mary has in Ireland's. Sunniva, the woman, has been silenced and permitted no space beyond the ascetic purity and mythical spirituality imposed on her. These poems are an attempt to liberate Sunniva from her story and give her a voice. Sunniva is reinvented as a sailor, a farmer and an exiled woman in search of a home.

In early 2020, I was awarded a mentorship by Munster Literature Centre with the US poet Paula Bohince. During this time, the Sunniva poems took shape and solidified. I would like to thank the Munster Literature Centre for the opportunity to concentrate on these poems and Paula Bohince for her considered advice. I would also like to thank Tony Ward and Angela Jarman of Arc Publications for having enough faith in my Sunniva poems to publish *Travellers of the North*..

PART I

SUNNIVA LONGS

I, Sunniva, am quite mad with longing.
To run wild as a boy in a streel of golden sun,
to run on into the cold drench of dark,
the air sharp with briars, apples, horse sweat.

My father all set jaw, my mother a quiver,
squares her shoulders yet smells of fear.
I swallow, resist contagion, I will not marry,
I cannot, I will not, I do not give consent.

Rosary beads clack the whispering wait,
the hushed sips and sighs of my mother.
Her loose threads of impatience I work
into a tapestry of dust, stillness, longing.

Alban, loyal brother, perfidious son,
please cleave to me, aid me, help my escape.
Let us conceive of, then weave a fine plot,
a sea way for me, Sunniva, to heave, leave, go.

SUNNIVA SETS FORTH

A portmanteau of ragged dreams,
a refusal of forced connubial haste,
one stern father, ready to disown.

A compass, a sextant, a bag of charms.
One mother, tearful, yet acquiescent,
accompaniment in the form of a brother.

On cold grey seas by sturdy currach.
As first light streaks the sky above,
we make to leave our only home.

Tears freeze in the tracks of the wind
as we set our watch for the borealis,
into the strange, cold *heimslige* North.

SICKNESS

In our naomhog, made from wicker and skin,
we are thrown about on the wild, wild seas.
Flung this way and that until my innards rattle,
the sky pales, the very sea turns to bile.

As I dry heave into the wild Northern waves,
Alban rows, watchful by night, vigilant by day.
My yellow-red eyes scan the sky for horizon.
In between bouts of sickness, there is slumber.

My fevered dreams are of the Mediterranean,
calm shores, the blood-orange ochre of France.
The silkest of seas takes me down, I slide down,
bisou, bienvenue, bisou, I ease down, blindfolded.

Into a mirage of lavender fields, douce, doucement,
the tarragon, timian, the vines, so lovely, chauteauy
in the brutal shortness of May, on through poplars,
birches, mimosa, to the rocks, scree of the Calanques.

NAVIGATION

I recover to learn navigation by the sun, moon, stars
with an instrument known as the kamal, a wonder
that measures latitudes and longitudes of the stars
gifted to Alban by a passing sailor from the Mahgreb.

A mere rough-hewn card, some string held between the teeth,
by which contrivance we find Polaris, then steer our way on.
Emboldened by this success, I vow to become a greater seaman
than any man of the sea – including Alban – could ever hope to be.

I adhere to the kamal, learn its ways on glassy flat-calm seas,
up England's coast, northwards to Scotland, from there to Orkney
whose green fields, golden sands lure us to stay a *peerie start*.
Branded interlopers, ferry loupers, we are refused leave to land.

OILEÁN NA MARBH

Oileán na marbh,
home of lost souls.
All our dreams were of you,
who would come to wake us.

Suicides, parricides, children
left unmarked, float now
in your murky, pagan hide.

All that time we dreamed
of you who would come to wake us.
You did not come.

Death came to us as easily
as rain drips into the silk
black welcome of the sea.

All that time we dreamed
of you who would come
to wake us.

You did not come

Beacons spread their light,
but the night torches
did not shine on us.

All that time we dreamed
of you who would come
to wake us.

You did not come.

Leave us now to our island
place apart, to move gently
back and forth with
all the dead things.

All our dreams were of you
who would come to wake us.
You did not come,
you did not come.

When you did come,
you came too late.

SEA TERRORS

1

The Njogel, half-sea creature, half-horse,
emerges as night falls from the cold waves
to do us no good. Only the threat of the knife,
the heat, iron, gods can dissuade him.

Nothing to stave off this unwieldy beast,
nothing to smite him with, save to say get back
in the name of Poseidon, Neptune, Aegir.
By the name of all the gods of the sea, get back.

In a flash of lightning over the crest of the waves,
he rears up, his hind legs obscured by surf,
then retreats, vanishes back into the Haaf
with the Tangi, the Finn-whals, the mar-folk,
the selki-folk, the sea trolls, sea trows,
Finn folk, all the sea beings, malevolent and fair.

2

Of all the hostile creatures that roam the seas,
one of the most terrible is the Draugen.
He haunts the seas as a headless fisherman
and he who sights him is blighted, doomed,
condemned to certain death that very day.

More fearful still is the Kraken, a vile creature
of scales, skins, a serpent whose numerous arms
will pull down a man and swallow him whole.
This delicious memory will drive it on to hunt,
kill, devour entire crews in its virulent attempt
to sate its boundless appetite for human flesh.

SHELTIE

We pitch up at Shetland, brown land of peat,
mountain, voe and fiddle, neither flute nor forest.
Deft Northern folk with hard, flint-sharp faces,
they burn, they clear, they fish, chisel and build.
Forges, longboats, carriages, stone forts, long houses
with no space for us, neither time nor tolerance for us,
where Harald Harfagre and Magnus Magnusson hold sway.
Oot you soothmoothers, you Irish bastards, go away.
A sweet wind takes us from Sumburgh to Bressay,
softer, more settled country, grey, smoke-filled.
We take down our sails, decide to drop anchor
to stop at its mossy banks to fish, plan, sit,
get our bearings, rest a *peerie start*, look out to sea.
We mend the sails and watch the seals basking
in the winter sunshine, hear their sensible barks.
For they are sensible creatures, they know our ways
as well as we know ourselves and look upon us benignly.
Unlike their human counterparts, they wish us no harm.

The hidden, hunted faces of the Sami,
tipped from the blood warmth of the flames.
Their tools, their knives taken, their magic
turned monochrome, flash-frozen to frame.
Scattered in the ash of black Novembers,
their bones, their reindeer, their myths,
unfolded in tapestries of colour
in lilted plumes of yoik – their lament,
caught again as the light and dark etches
upon bare Kautokeino steppes.
Beautiful wild travellers of the North,
you're crazy, you drink, and you fight.
Your spells, secret knowledge and sorcery
waft still in the drifts of Arctic night.

LOFOTEN

A gale hurls us up against stone, stops us in our tracks,
forces us to make sudden landfall, to seek refuge,
sanctuary from the searing cold, the sharp bite of hail,
the fearsome wind that drowns our voices, makes us unheard
by the strange people, their closed, impassive faces,
muffled against the grey, frozen wall of Lofoten.

As strange as the people are, there are familiar creatures,
arctic skuas we have learned from the Shetland skies.
They call them bonxies. Puffins, sea eagles, cormorants,
eider ducks, terns we know as visitors to our own mild land.
Curlews, osprey, oystercatchers, lapwings, ruff, whimbrel,
whooper swans, black swans, all more at home than we
will ever be in this strange and frightening tundra of the north.

There are pole cats, lynxes, porpoises, otters of land and sea,
not to mention the whales great, blue, sperm, killer, orca.
The mighty humpback, whose eerie heartscald of a song,
a terrible, lonesome wail from beneath the waves, makes music
so strange that it causes the bowels of passing boats to quake.
Salted fishermen stop, take pause and question life itself.

SELJA

Flat calm after the storms of the open seas,
the gales, the howling winds, the tempests,
weary, unsettled seas, most fretful seas.
Biting salt lacerates, cuts, gouges our faces
until we would quit over and over again

if we could, loyal brother, but we cannot.
We must drive on, until we find a place
to stop, among folk that will tolerate us,
not throw us out, nor fight us, nor spurn,
thwart our quest to build ourselves a home.

We push on until we find the blessed shelter,
the cool embrace of the fjords, calm, elongated.
They soothe our weary spirits; still, cold, deep,
they speak to us kindly, will us to carry on.

At night, the foghorns in the brief darkness,
make not a ripple in the river of stars above.
The Hardanger fiddle shimmers, the curlew calls
all daylight night long; at dawn a luxuriant wallow
of seals smiles on us, coaxes us to stay a while.

In Selja we have found a place of sanctuary
where we can dream, build, dare to plant again.
So bleached, dried-out, bone weary are we
from the vicious winds, the terrible thirst,
the sun that burns on the angry, restless sea.

PART II

PART I

LENGE SIDEN SIST

Lenge siden sist, a long time since,
the thump of sliothar on hurl.
The drone of the pipes,
the cheers of the boys,
the kestrel's swoop and swirl.

Lenge siden sist, a long time since
we bid our one home farewell.
Chicks as we were when we left
our poor mother tearful, bereft.

Does she dare to say our names
to the stars, Ursa Major, Little Bear?
Pray the wind to carry sounds to us
of home gone a long time since.

The thump of sliothar on hurl.
The drone of the pipes,
the cheers of the boys,
the kestrel's swoop and swirl.

PLANTING

How I miss the shovels of home,
the soft, brown fullness of earth
wriggling and seething with life,
mud that would stick and clump,
bloom, spread like proven bread.

Here we must break backs, stones, earth,
to make beds where goats can barely graze.
Plant by the moon before the freeze
while there is light, golden, sepia-tinted.

As it waxes, plant hardy plants that grow above the soil,
kale, collards, carrots, leeks, no-nonsense plants,
sturdy enough to survive the bitter Arctic cold.
When the moon wanes, plant those that grow below,
tubers to prosper stealthily under cover of snow.

HOLY WOMAN

The word has spread that I am a holy woman,
who has embraced chastity, a mystic
whose solitary ways speak of holiness sublime.

I am not pious, I know nothing of god,
save the spirits that inhabit both land and sea.
Yet I will use this power to curb unruly ways,
calm the Norsemen, let them work the land for me.

They come to settle, bring their sheep from the mainland,
their longhorn cattle, goats and pigs from neighbouring Kinn.
I keep to my cave, anxious, not knowing how to manage
this burly crew of Norse, would-be Christian men.

To repel them would be folly, to encourage them more so,
for I dare not displease Jarl Haakon nor provoke his ire.
The word is out that he accuses me of stealing sheep,
to rouse the rage of his band of bloodied, fighting men.

My holy name may keep me safe, a reputation for godliness
adheres to me although I do not know a god in any shape or form.
It seems a woman who lives alone must be a bride of Christ.
If she is not the bride of any other, then she is shackled to him.

Christ will get all glory for what I build here in my own right
which is most galling to me as I have struggled to plough
my own furrow here on Selja, to sow seeds in the right spot,
await the green shoots in spring, lay down hay for my pullets.

The fruits of my labours will be ascribed to wonders, miracles,
not to my hard work, my ice-hacking, back-breaking graft,
my rising at five to dig, pull stones out of the frozen earth,
scrape away weeds, dig, hoe, so that my plants, my life, thrive.

SHEEP-STEALING WHORE

Sheep-stealing whore, bitch.
Who does she think she is?
We should have run her,
driven the barbarian
double crosser from our shore.
Instead we let her in,
a woman unaccompanied,
unhusbanded harlot, sneak.
Some say she is an Irish noble,
unwelcome in her own home.
Others say she is a holy woman,
a mystic who starves in a cave.
We believe it not, she has no god.
We will drive her from our shore,
witch, sheep-stealing Irish whore.

A FATHER'S FURY

That will be your last refusal, Sunniva, my girl.
The Jarl, upon my orders, will sack, then raze Selja,
kill every last man, sheep on it, then take you away,
my Sunniva, to where the women will protect you,
from your old father's anger, I pray.

I wish the Jarl godspeed in this work, good luck.
He will be paid in gold to restore my honour and fortune.
My Sunniva, it is not too late to marry you to a knave,
let you earn back what you stole, repent your ingrate ways.
I will not punish your forever. Yet, you must obey.

Alban, my impudent, deceitful son, I will leave to his fate,
and his Viking wench and bastard child – if they survive Selja's sack,
for it is unlikely my first-born will fight off the Jarl's men.
I have not ordered his capture, but they may kill him for jest.
It concerns me not. It is my daughter Sunniva I will have back.

A LEMMING YEAR

I happened upon a lemming year.
Coming upon a glut, an agitation
Of furred puffballs, screaming
their terror and rage
against the mountainside.

I saw one almost implode,
so sharp and urgent was its fury
as if it knew – how could it
have known? – its fate would be
decided in that fourth year

by the black fjord below.
How would it tackle it?
If it could tackle it at all
and if it came up short
timing would be everything

I could not have known what
lay before me in that lemming year.
It raged all the same,
making angry, ineffectual pleas
to the icy, blue mountain

And what of the others?
Do lemmings get survivor guilt?

THE DEPTHS

We hear the shouts late evening as the wind drops.
Come to attack women, farmers, no need for stealth.
Night falls quietly, too quickly, the stream of stars
above my place of refuge, no comfort now, no hope.

The oars we have feared so long coming on the sea
dip deep, strike as one rough splash as the savages
make for our placid shores. Alban and I, gentle Liv,
their milky child, must make haste, run to hide.

They will dash our brains out, fling us into the sea,
laugh as the waves divide us, send us to a lonely grave.
I would rather dally with a sea monster for all eternity
than spend one minute with a brute in the Jarl's pay.

They make landfall with a roar, chase the poor souls
too slow to run. We roll a boulder across its mouth,
delay their access to my cave, damp, dark sanctuary,
our only refuge in this tiny place of moss and stones.

Screams rip through the earth, those poor shepherds,
their women, babes, sheep, left behind to face death.
O slaughtered innocents, they will not live to look
at daylight again, walk in a Selja, mad alive in spring.

We cower ten-fold in our cave, squeeze, press forward
in one heave, force ourselves down, down, down
through cloying passages where we have never been,
where nisse live and trolls, creatures turned to stone.

A deep, dark rumble fills us with fresh terror. The thud
of heavy boots, we shake, gasp, tremble; is it the Jarl's men?
Thunder peal or rockfall, we know it to be our last ordeal.
As the earth's walls fall in around us, we choke for breath,
our mouths, throats, eyes fill with dust, we can no more.

TO HAUNT YOU

If I do come back to haunt you
it will be in winter in your darkest time.
I will lead you through frozen pathways,
make a trail of silver so you know
to follow me down to a patched field
by a shallow river, half-frozen.
We will lie there beneath the surface
to warm the stones,
petrified until the thaw when I will lead
you through the scree, up a cinder path
to a small house by the side of a fjord
with a log pile outside, waiting
for you to follow me through a forest
of pine to a summerhouse shuttered
against the heat, where I will close a door
behind us, a heavy, wooden door.

SUNNIVA

For Sunniva, your glory,
is not dead.

My life sings still
in the ocean waves,
the sky and the stars.

I have escaped the dark cave
where fate would wall me in
with my prayers.

I do not pray, I will not pray.

The sea bleaches my bones,
brings me closer to home.
Soon I will be translated.

Yet I cannot forget the rain,
the sharp bite of hail,
the salt wind on my face.

The violet of the borealis
as the blood-red moon pulls
silver fish back and forth.

NOTES

p. 14 - *heimslige:* like home

p. 15 - *naomhog:* a traditional Irish boat with a wooden frame over which animal hides or skins were stretched.
- *timian:* thyme in Norwegian

p. 16 - *peerie start:* a short while in Shetland dialect.
- *ferry loupers:* non-native inhabitants of Orkney who crossed the Pentland Firth from the mainland by ferry.

p. 17
- *Oileán na marbh:* Originally named Island of the Sea / Oileán na Mara, the tragic history that befell this tiny island at Carrickfinn over the centuries led to its gradual name change to Oileán na Marbh, Island of the Dead.

p. 19 - *Haaf:* deep-sea fishing ground off the Shetland and Orkney islands.
- *Tangi:* water spirit in Shetland folk-lore
- *Sea trows:* a loose designation in the Shetland Isles for sea-beings of any kinds (including mermen and selki-folk). A sea-trow can also take the form of a woman whose wailing cries, when heard at sea by fishermen usually portend sorrow or distress.

p.20 - *voe:* a small bay or creek in Orkney or Shetland.

p. 21 - *Sami:* a people speaking the Sami language and inhabiting Lapland and adjacent areas of northern Norway, Sweden, and Finland, as well as the Kola Peninsula of Russia. In Norway, the Sami people live in almost all parts of Northern Norway, and in the some southern parts of the country.
- *yoik:* a traditional form of song in Sámi music.

p. 27 - *sliothar:* a hard solid sphere slightly larger than a tennis ball, consisting of a cork core covered by two pieces of leather stitched together.

p. 29 - *Kinn:* an island off the coast of Norway.

p. 31 - *Jarl:* Old Norse for 'chieftain', particularly a chieftain set to rule a territory in a king's stead.

p. 33 - *nisse:* a mythological creature from Nordic folklore associated with the winter solstice.

Fiona Smith is an Irish poet whose work has been published in *Crannog, Dreich, Hennessy New Irish Writing Poetry Ireland Review, The Stony Thursday Book, Southword* and the anthologies *Skein* (Templar Poetry, 2014) and *Over the Edge – The First Ten Years* (Salmon Poetry, 2013). She was selected for a *Poetry Ireland* workshop with Eavan Boland at Kilkenny Arts Festival in 2018 and was also selected to be mentored by the John Montague fellow Paula Bohince in early 2020 at the Munster Literature Centre.

She has read at the Derwent Arts Festival, Cork Spring Poetry Festival, Skibbereen Arts Festival and Kinsale Arts Festival and at Charlie Byrne's bookshop and the Crane pub in Galway. She has also read at Cork's poetry event Ó Bheal.

In her capacity as the voluntary poetry coordinator for Kinsale Arts since 2019, she has arranged readings with poets including Bernard O'Donoghue, Leanne O'Sullivan and for the 2022 event, Paul Muldoon.